Becoming Naked

Peter Lay

Black Eyes Publishing UK

Becoming Naked
© Peter Lay, 2022

Cherry Blossom
© Peter Lay & Motoko Sorano, 2022

Published in 2022
Black Eyes Publishing UK
34 Stocken Close
Hucclecote, Gloucester
GL3 3UL (UK)

www.blackeyespublishinguk.co.uk

ISBN: 9781913195168

A CIP catalogue record for this title is available from
the British Library.

First Edits: Carol Sheppard

Final Edits: Josephine Lay

The only potential for immortality
resides amongst the living

Becoming Naked

Contents

Becoming Naked

Cherry Blossom (with Motoko Sorano)

Mouse will hide away when the Ox comes...

Zaiming Wang

For Zaiming with love, wherever life takes you...

It's cold on the mountain
without the warmth
of the yellow flower.

The gardener has retired
to a chair beside a window
and the weeds are sprouting

The bear is hibernating
snoring loudly
in a deep, deep sleep

The milk lady ran away with the ox
making babies
in distant lands

The yellow flower
is no longer seen on the mountain
The terrain is cold and bleak.

Mix

In another world,
in another time
there would be a long
line of perfume bottles.

L'Air du Temps,
Beautiful,
Opium.

Now that would be
a strange mix
and a heady scent.

Cemetery

The headstone on the grave;
Maria Lay
24th April 1955 – 9th December 1990
'Remembered with Happiness'

I stand staring at this new stone,
a replacement of the badly weathered one
I've looked at for 26 years
and reflect on echoes from the past…

Stonehenge, South Shields,
the beach in Menorca.
I remember conception, birth,
the quiet day at Mallards Pike Lake
just before losing you.

I'm torn to see this shiny black monolith
with gold lettering
the words repeated…
'Remembered with Happiness'.
I place red flowers against the black.

You are not here under the stone,
your ashes are in a box
at the bottom of this plot
under my feet.

I always sense that if I look up
I might see you
out of the corner of my eye,

in the distance
watching me...

So, I scan the horizon for sight of you -
but which of you,
there are two...

This white stone set
in a diamond cremation plot
has your ashes beneath. It reads;
Helen Predgen-Lay
16th March 1965 – 4th June 2010.
'A great influence on the lives of many,
a truly remarkable woman'.

I remember Javea and Moraira in Spain,
Ilfracombe Youth Arts Festival,
your new car, your fear of heights.
Again, conception and birth,
before your past took hold,
only releasing you with your last breath.

I place yellow flowers against the white –
yellow roses for Helen,
red roses or freesia's for Maria
some 200 metres away…

I scan the horizon for sight of you
but which of you
there are two...

But which of you
there are two of you...

Perhaps walking
arm in arm
in the distance,
watching me,
the two of you.

Boots Magic

In a Wiltshire field
not far from Avebury…
is buried a boot,
well two boots actually,
two red boots
Dr Martens

Under the turf they lie
deep in the earth,
buried
down deep, watered
as the rain falls…

We were walking
across Charles Bridge
in Prague, she said
'When you've finished
with those boots,
can I have them?'
I looked at her, *Why?*
and she sang, *Nai nana nai*

We walked around
the stone circle at Avebury
in the dark of night,
her dress floating sensually
in the breeze
I looked at her, *Why?*
and she sang, *Nai nana nai*

In a Wiltshire field
not far from Avebury…
is buried a boot,
well two boots actually,
two red boots
Dr Martens

Under the turf they lie
deep in the earth,
buried
down deep, watered
as the rain falls…

Venice Carnival 1995

A cascade of colourful costume
men dressed as women, women as men.
Me in my red Dr Martens
you in your short skirt
wearing our new Venetian masks.
Others in historical long dresses
mix with ghosts from the past
clustered on bridges
over canals.

The opera; a romantic gondola ride;
coffee in Piazza San Marco,
the entrance to the Basilica,
covered by inches of water.
Dragon Masks; Chinese stilt walkers;
Looking for gaps in the crowds
to photograph the array
of history and outlandish fantasy.

Away from the bustling piazza
the lens captures transitory figures.

One photo taken of an empty scene
when developed
showed a person dressed in yellow
with a yellow crown.

Bayeux at night

our bodies in heat
loving with intensity
and carnal desire

In between
nocturnally sleeping
in the car
or on the bathroom floor

Then wandering the street
slipping from doorway
to doorway
moving languidly

Looking at the window displays
of art
and a picture
we bought many years later.

We are penned

sometimes unsheathed
to spill the words, we create
by bringing forth the ink
inside us

At other times we are closed
shut with a click
no words can be completed
until we become open again

Sometimes we are in love
sliding in and out of the cap
keeping the ink moist from drying
from too much exposure.

Standing in Ecuador 1

It takes two days to adjust
to the high altitude of Quito

14 miles north of the city
is the 'Middle of the World';
The Equator both of them…
Confused?

Prior to the invention
of accurate GPS,
in 1736, an expedition led by
Charles-Marie de La Condamie
pinpointed the location
of the Equator.

A 100-foot tall, monument
was erected - Mitad Del Mundo
It's where most of the tourists
from Quito come
to stand astride the yellow line
for the classic one foot
in each hemisphere shot.

The fact is
the line is out by 240 metres
but don't let that get in the way
of that obligatory photo,
click.

However, as you leave the Mitad del Mundo
turn left, go uphill
and follow the signs
for the Museum de Sitio Intinan

Here you'll find interactive displays;
exhibits about Ecuadorian indigenous culture;
totem poles, real shrunken heads
and the body of an enormous dead snake.

It is welcoming, and lots of fun
you can balance an egg on a nail,
watch water swirling in different directions
on either side of the equator,
And lots more….

And of course, you can stand astride
a mix of brick and ochre painted line,
the real Equator,
to take that classic one foot
in each hemisphere,
obligatory photo,
click.

Standing in Ecuador 2

I stand in Cotopaxi National Park
at 11,200 feet
posing in front of the active,
stratovolcano, Cotopaxi
that rises 8,200 feet above me
and steams…
Click!
Asombroso!
Awesome…

Cotopaxi last erupted in 2016,
yet the slopes are still closed to the public…

Later we stand
with our legs astride
the source of the Amazon,
(well, one of the sources)
as it crosses a field
and runs down a gully
by the side of the road.
Click.

We stop for a lunch
of grilled fish, potatoes and salad.
We look through telescopes
at the majestic condors spiralling
over far-off cliffs.

Then we gasp as, one bird
banks low over the roof of a low,
wooden building just a few metres from us
before soaring away.

There are less than one hundred
wild, Andean, condors
left in Ecuador.

Amazon

the greatness of nature has only two weapons:
a river and a woman.
The smile is the seal
at the foot of its destiny.

amazona
by AZEL (Benito Rosales) for Sofiama

la grandeza de la naturaleza solo tiene dos armas
un río, una mujer
la sonrisa es el sello lacrado
al pie de su destino.

This is an ekphrastic poem by AZEL (Benito Rosales) that was inspired by a photograph clicked in Standing in Ecuador 2

September

Waking, rising, and walking
in the early morning glow
I saw golden leaves
                    falling,
                            tumbling
into Autumn

What of Summer?

I blinked and...

Bare

Perhaps…

We can celebrate
when we meet
with food and fun,
express our feelings
with frenzy and laughter
to ease your pain.

To maybe gain
a pause –
in an oasis
where time stands still.

Just you and I
shedding the clothes of our minds
becoming naked in thought.

Inter-Continental

I slip out of my dream,
to go to the bathroom.

I come out of the bathroom
and I'm in your house.

I tip toe to your room,
quietly so as not to wake
your husband

and slip into your bed

Impressions

As I photograph you
in your naked beauty,
the lens captures
every exquisite detail,

like a lover penetrating
you with passion.

The Intimacy of the Grand Old Duke of York

Intimacy is about
lips, touch and connection...
The intensity
of skin against skin...
But when a man faces
the difficult understanding
that he can no longer perform
like a young man...
Age and ailments
taking their toll.

I think of the
Grand Old Duke of York...
When they were up
they were up...
When they were down
they were down...
And when they were only half way up
they were neither up nor down...

The Sounds of a Symphonic Gong –
Interpreting Typhoon Hagibis.

At 11:32am on 27th October 2019.

Ziggy wears a hat
sits enlightening, while manspreading
and twiddling his thumbs.

The hands on the clock say 12:35.
Silver armour over a white dress
stands on a table   headless.

Tattooed forearms accentuate
explanations by hand and mouth,
'Leave a space for filling later
focus on sight   sound and smell'

The Symphonic Gong begins at 11:52am.
Though the clock says five to one.

An earthquake rumbles
like a shinkansen flashing through stations.
The subtle roar crescendos,
echoing into the distance.

A performance or a call to prayers?

Fuji-san sits majestic
as the tornado rips through streets
scattering debris and light.

Hagibis has come!
Its rhythm pulsates through the destruction,

while the 'Cherry Blossoms'
weave their magic with slick
hand to hand passing at devastating speed.

In the background...

Shrine bells
Samurai swords clashing
buildings crashing.

Noise fading.

The sun rests on the arm of a sofa.
I drink green tea and slurp udon.

It's 12:03pm.

Chiba's mayor makes an award
to Motoko san

the clock says 1:06pm.

Typhoon Hagibis (4 Oct– 13 Oct 2019) - a large, powerful tropical cyclone, considered to be the most devastating typhoon to hit the Kantō region of Japan since Ida in 1958. Hagibis caused additional impact to Japan, a month after Typhoon Faxai.

It was followed by heavy rain causing increased flooding and mud-slides.

An earthquake magnitude 5.7 also occurred in the Kantō region on the evening of the 12th October 2019.

The 'Cherry Blossoms' is the nickname of the Japanese Rugby Team who were playing in the Rugby World Cup in Japan.

My Talent

I have a gift:
the gift of sleep.
It is my gift
given to me.

Time Zones

Where do all those hours go
as we pass between time zones
falling?
Never seen by those below.

They exist only in aeroplanes.

I am sad

that life is so difficult for you...
I don't know how to make it better...

I would reach for you
hold you close
kiss you
love you

But I know it's no longer your desire...

But, how can I be bored
when you bite me
Roy Orbison sings in the background
my body aches with desire.

Ideas

In Sengaku-Ji to honour the 47 Ronin
my mind remembers everything
and nothing.

Nothing exists in a vacuum
and Zaira sings...
I believe in you...

My ears strain
for the lost words
At least I can still eat chocolate
and you don't have to be able to spell bricks to lay them.

There are no coincidences
So, love me till the angel's cry.

A fondness for opera is revealing
Life is for the living
Don't waste a moment

Humans can love more than one person at a time
I long gave up on the thought of monogamy
That is not to say I intend to be promiscuous.

Heartbreaking

A beautiful bride draped
in white wedding gown
poses for pictures

The camera zooms in…

Beirut is decimated
by an explosion –
a detonation of tons of ammonium nitrate
that has sat unsecured
in a portside warehouse
for years.
Lebanon's capital is devasted
Hundreds killed; thousands injured.

Her beautiful moment rips into horror.
Flowers are torn from the ground
the white dress billows.
The blast
sweeps through the square.

And the bride and her party,
dash for safety
amid clouds of dust and debris.
Incredibly none are badly hurt

The bride gathers up her skirts
runs to treat the injured,
as the doctor she is.

Shiver

1

I will whisper in your ears
and make you shiver

In my mind
I am my younger self
gazing at your beauty.
My desire takes hold
I want to love you
to hear you sing
your voice reminds me
of the sweet scent of lilies.

I see you in May
by the stream under the trees
among the blooming white roses –
pure innocent, obedient flowers
like girls with buds for breasts
breathing softly in the shade
reciting poems of unrequited love
whilst surrounded by tall trees
dark and melancholy.

2

You ripen into womanhood
teacher, wife and mother
I know you from these pictures
and your words.
Every memory you share,
every photograph, takes me there
as though I was behind the lens
I know these are your memories
I'm sharing
but each one makes me desire
to be there.

3

When we first met
your long black hair
entangled me in a short embrace
hunger and desire
on a bed of Cherry blossom
no longer innocent

Much later we loved
we laughed and kissed
We watched Sumo and Kabuki
We slept naked
entwined in each-other's arms
under the enchantment of Hagoromo.

4

Time passes
I travel to your door once more
We summon up
all the passion of our lives
All that has gone before
was a rehearsal
for this time together.
We cry with the emotion
of Nagasaki and Hiroshima
The beauty of Miyajima
and are swept away
by the art of Naoshima

We make beautiful music together
and cry out with the intensity of it.

5

Amid the shadow of Covid-19,
All travel is postponed...
For us, no pre-olympic journey
to Sendai,
a city with beautiful zelkova trees
lining its main streets.

We will not reach Matsushima
with its many tiny offshore islands
covered in pines

We will not visit Morioka,
the hometown of
Takuboku Ishikawa, aka Woodpecker
The Japanese poet who died of tuberculosis
at the age of 26.

Will we ever dance naked in the snow?
That story hasn't yet been written.

6

We cannot stop running
running
running
and running...

Until the end of our lives
cherry blossom will always be in our hearts
and beneath our feet

forever.

42 Days to Japan

*42, is my favourite number; the meaning of life, and yesterday, it was 42
days to my flight to Japan.*

Confined in my prison
with crap television
a strange dystopian view
of deserted streets
beyond the window,
unknown futures of friends, family
and distant lovers.

Sunshine brightens the mood
as we get into the garden
patching up next door's fence
broken after the storms
and left.

Our cat, Charlotte,
is frightened
by the gap in her domain
so, we fill it
temporarily, in the sun.

Now, I'm speaking words
as I zoom before of a sea of faces,
a map of Japan behind me.

Two crows in the garden
black and menacing
are moving in
on a pair of magpies.

Dancing Naked in Snow

I feel confined - claustrophobic
shut in - imprisoned

My life is here
as well as elsewhere,
Japan, Quito, Ecuador,
France, Spain
and the Netherlands
Manchester, Swindon, Rugby,
Surrey and Stoke-on-Trent.

I Skype, Zoom
and Messenger video chat.

Use WhatsApp, email and text.
But I long for the open road
the open skies
your hugs and kisses.

For a time when we finally
dance naked in snow?

Adjourned

I look forward to our
eagerly anticipated date
by the sea,
at a time up for discussion
up in the air;
to be decided,
but as yet, unspecified.

At some point
in the near
or distant future,
will be brought to a conclusion
as the matters causing doubt
are resolved.

So, whilst this determination
to meet is continually desired,
again, it still cannot be decided
at this moment
in time, so,

we wait...

Naked

I stand at the window
stripped of my humanity
dreams shredded

no thoughts beyond today

except poetry
September nine
online
amidst grey skies.

Silent Rain

The rain is a curtain of soft wet beads
Soundless to the deaf.

No way of expressing this aspect
of being wet...

Life is full of choices,

Coffee or tea
You and me
Roti's, parathas
Fish and chips
Hot or cold
Yes or no

But…
Black and white
should be combined
with no divide.

Thoughts

If you have a moment,
I would share my thoughts with you

Life is full of compromise
in dealings and relationships

But, never in the thoughts
and feelings with oneself.

Time

Time is an illusion

If there is no rush...
If you have the will

then what is desired
will come to be.

In time

I awake, thinking
about yesterday
Difficult conversation
about expectations;
patterns of behaviour;
fuelled by the past.
Like music
on constant repeat.

I like to think
we can break that mould
create a gentle, equal
appreciation of life
and love
out of mutual respect.

And yes, passion
in our eyes,
in our words,
in our closeness,

through time.

The Dance

First time

your eyes
and blue eyes
ignite
in a kiss.

I want to go to Avebury

I am fed up with this situation.
Filled with irritation.

I want to feel
with my hands
the power of stones

to be one with the Universe.

Hi

Sorry
I couldn't make the group.

Doing a lot of Zoom.
Considering our plight
our possible doom.

In Lockdown
time flies and drags.
Did this; did that…
Or at least meant to.

I thought of you,
your energetic walks
around the coast.
Your nocturnal escapades
with fallen trees.

I miss our talks
the coffee and cake
in cafes.

Earth

The climate is out of control.

We have ravaged the earth
and now it is fighting back.

It will consume the innocent
as well as the guilty...

Another

another day.
A Friday
slips by
uneventful
predictable.

Saturday is coming
with a hint of snow.

Somewhere New

I have a list.
A list that will never be completed,
but never fully deleted.

I've never been to the City of Cadiz –
famous for its many watchtowers
scattered around the city
its beautiful beaches
the sunny climate.
And for posing as Cuba
in James Bond's, *Die Another Day*

I wish to take you there:
to the small atmospheric city
to walk the narrow, cobbled streets,
eat tapas on street corners
enjoy 'flamenco' –
and the rhythm of guitars.

Revel in its beauty
kiss under the stars.

Ancient stones

take me back
to a time

when lovers united
inside the circle
felt grass
under their backs.

While custodians of the woods

stood still
upon the ground
tall and straight
amidst unkempt paths.

Both silent guardians.

Jump

Jump naked
into the pool of enlightenment
and feel the universe envelop you.

Take My Hand

Take my hand
Walk with me for a while

Excuse my limp
It is improving

I can't hear your voice
It's just a whisper

My eyes miss your smiles.

Doughnuts

Lily,
celebrates the arrival
of her super-charged,
super-fast,
electric wheelchair.

Skirts flying
She does doughnuts
in the garden.

Hooked

Feel the wind
in your skirts
The lashes of rain
on your skin
Dancing close
surrendering to the rhythm,
the pulsating beat,
the vocal hook.

Aging

Aging is a strange concept
to one who is immortal.

A concept and understanding
that immortality is fragile,
not forever,

and one day will cease to be,
one will cease to be,
cease to be immortal,
cease to be.

Words

Sometimes
words spoken
are stronger
than verse written.

Cherry Blossom

A small collection of Japan inspired poems

by

Peter Lay & Motoko Sorano

Ueno Park Today

Ueno Park today
is without cherry blossom
where it once overflowed

A single blossom
of cherry dances in wind
lost in the labyrinth.

A cherry blossom
is so sweet and rare in the
Autumn of the year.

When cherry blossom
is bruised it's still beautiful
and smells as sweet.

Morning

Under the morning
sun, the cherry blossom sits
In peaceful harmony

When I am with you
the sound of the waterfall
purifies my heart

I think Cherry Blossom nectar
must be the sweetest
thing I have tasted.

Wonderful

It is wonderful
to see the cherry blossom
while sipping green tea

The simplicity of cherry blossom
offers a rich complexity
that is deeply metaphorical.

Among shades of pink
my favourite tint will be
one, the sweetest red.

Sky

In the heart
I harbour the sky
Peacefully.

Spring

On a Spring day
The skylark sings her
Peaceful song.

Reflection

Under a pine tree 300 years old
Far away from Chiba,
Let's take a look at the extraordinary world
For a moment of peace.

At the site of Takamatsu castle

Early morning walk
Shadow of a pine shining in a pond
Feel peace in a quiet atmosphere
A pleasant breeze touches my cheek.

At Ritaurin Park

In the fresh morning air
Sitting on a large stone in the garden
hearing birds sing

In front of me,
the orange and pink of azaleas.

My heart fills with sweet chocolate

I want to write some words
and whisper them softly
into your ear

I opened the door
to see morning glory flowers
as I expected

Finally
I touch them
I take in their scent

Take their picture.

Cherry Blossom

Fluttering
Falling cherry blossoms by the wind
How fleeting flowers are!

Wake Butterfly

inspired by an original Japanese Haiku, by Matsuo Bashō (1644-1694)

wake butterfly, wake butterfly
it is late my love
come fly with me.

By Peter Lay

Becoming Naked (2022)

Still Tilting at Windmills (2019)

redbootsman 'Such Strange Philosophies' (2016)

~

By Peter Lay & Zaiming Wang

Yellow Over The Mountain (2018)
岭上黄

Another Friday (2019)

Peter Lay

The essence of living is to enjoy each moment unchained to the past with no concern for the future. It is not that you negate the past or never plan for the future but there are times when you should abandon yourself to the moment.

I am like a Sybarite – my brain is hard-wired into my sensory perceptions. Each touch of my fingers on the soft flesh of my love, brings exquisite pleasure. The thrill of texture and smoothness; of moisture and movement – to caress, to be caressed, is happiness beyond compare.

This is my heaven and I want no more – immortality does not attract or concern me for I can't conceive of an existence without my body; without its senses, without taste, without art, music and love, and the perfumes of life and the richness derived from them.

I would like to dedicate this book to all the women who have inspired the writing of these poems.

CPSIA information can be obtained
at www.ICGtesting.com
Printed in the USA
BVHW061547261222
654958BV00017B/1008

9 781913 195168